Mel Bay's
BEST OF BACH
FOR CLASSIC GUITAR
Edited by Joseph Castle

PREFACE

The music of Bach lends itself particularly well to transcriptions for guitar. This is perhaps true because much of Bach's keyboard music was written to be played on the harpsichord or kindred instruments in which the strings are plucked by tiny quills called plectra. The strings of a guitar are made to sound in much the same manner except that fingers cause the strings to vibrate instead of quills mounted on wooden jacks. Thus the tone of the two types of instruments is somewhat similar.

Another reason Bach's music is interesting played on the guitar is that it is written in contrapuntal style. Because of this, even a Minuet in just two voices is enjoyable to listen to.

The pieces in this volume are especially well suited for teaching or public performance.

Joseph Castle

CONTENTS

	page
Minuet	1
March	2
Minuet	3
Chorale	4
Minuet	5
Courante	6
Sleeper's Awake	8
Air For The G String	10
Gavotte-from 6th Sonata for Solo Violin	12
Courante-from Suite No. 3 for Cello	15

© 2008, 1977 BY MEL BAY PUBLICATIONS, INC., PACIFIC, MO 63069.
ALL RIGHTS RESERVED. INTERNATIONAL COPYRIGHT SECURED. B.M.I. MADE AND PRINTED IN U.S.A.
No part of this publication may be reproduced in whole or in part, or stored in a retrieval system, or transmitted in any form or by any means, electronic, mechanical, photocopy, recording, or otherwise, without written permission of the publisher.

Visit us on the Web at www.melbay.com — E-mail us at email@melbay.com

In the little town of Eisenach, Germany, Johann Sebastian Bach first saw the light of day on the 21st of March, 1685. With at least fifty musical relatives in his family, it is no wonder that he took to music as soon as he could talk.

Bach's whole life was devoted to music. He was an intensely religious person and music, to Bach, was a means of worship.

Bach was a family man. With the help of two successive wives, a jolly family of twenty children were reared, to whom he was as kindly as his elders had been severe with him.

The following Minuet is one of the many pieces Bach wrote as teaching material for his children.

MINUET

Johann Sebastian Bach
(1685 – 1750)

Allegretto

The young Bach received his earliest systematic instruction on keyboard instruments from an elder brother.

An interesting story illustrates the younger boy's intense interest in music. Behind his brother's bookshelf was a large volume of pieces by German composers. He was refused permission to use the book, so he copied it out by moonlight, completing the task in six months.

The March which follows is from a group of pieces entitled "Clavier Book for Anna Magdalena Bach" which Bach wrote as teaching material for his second wife.

MARCH

MINUET

In its earliest form, the Minuet consisted of two eight measure phrases, each of which was repeated. Each phrase usually began on the first beat of the measure, but occasionally we find one starting on the third. Beethoven's famous "Minuet In G" is an exception to the general rule.

The following Minuet is from the "Clavier Book for Anna Magdalena Bach." It follows the Classic Form.

The word "Clavier" is the French name for nearly any keyboard instrument such as the harpsichord, organ, clavichord, or piano.

Allegretto

CHORALE

Bach left to posterity 371 four-voiced chorale tunes, all enriched with his matchless harmonizations. In the majority of cases the melodies are those from the vast number that were in current use by the Lutheran Church. These melodies were derived from secular (folksongs), Gregorian chants, and songs that originated within the church itself.

This chorale is entitled "Dir, dir, Jehovah, will ich singen" which, translated, means "To Thee, Jehovah, I Will Sing."

MINUET

Bach began his professional career at about age fifteen, at which time he took a position with the principal choir of Mettenschüler.

Even at this early age, Bach had an insatiable quest for knowledge and more than once walked thirty miles and back to hear the veteran organist, Johann Reinken, who held a position in Hamburg.

This Minuet is another of those contained in a volume of pieces entitled "Clavier Book for Anna Magdalena Bach."

Allegretto

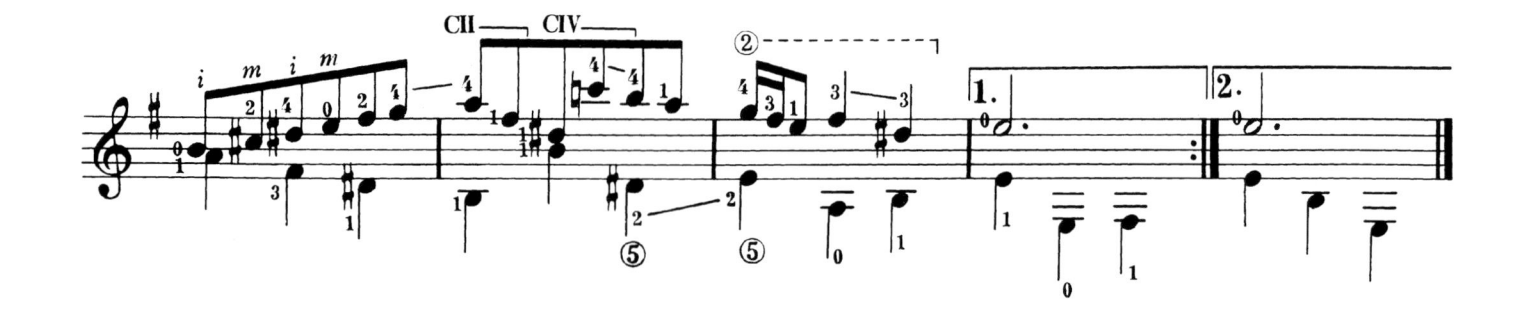

COURANTE

The Courante is a dance of French origin. The word, Courante, literally means to run, or running. It was greatly in vogue during the 17th century. It attained its greatest popularity during the reign of Louis XIV, who was King of France from 1643 to 1715.

Like most of the other old style dances, the Courante consists of two parts, each of which is usually repeated. Bach made extensive use of courante movements in suites for keyboard instruments as well as for solo violin and solo cello.

Allegro ma non troppo

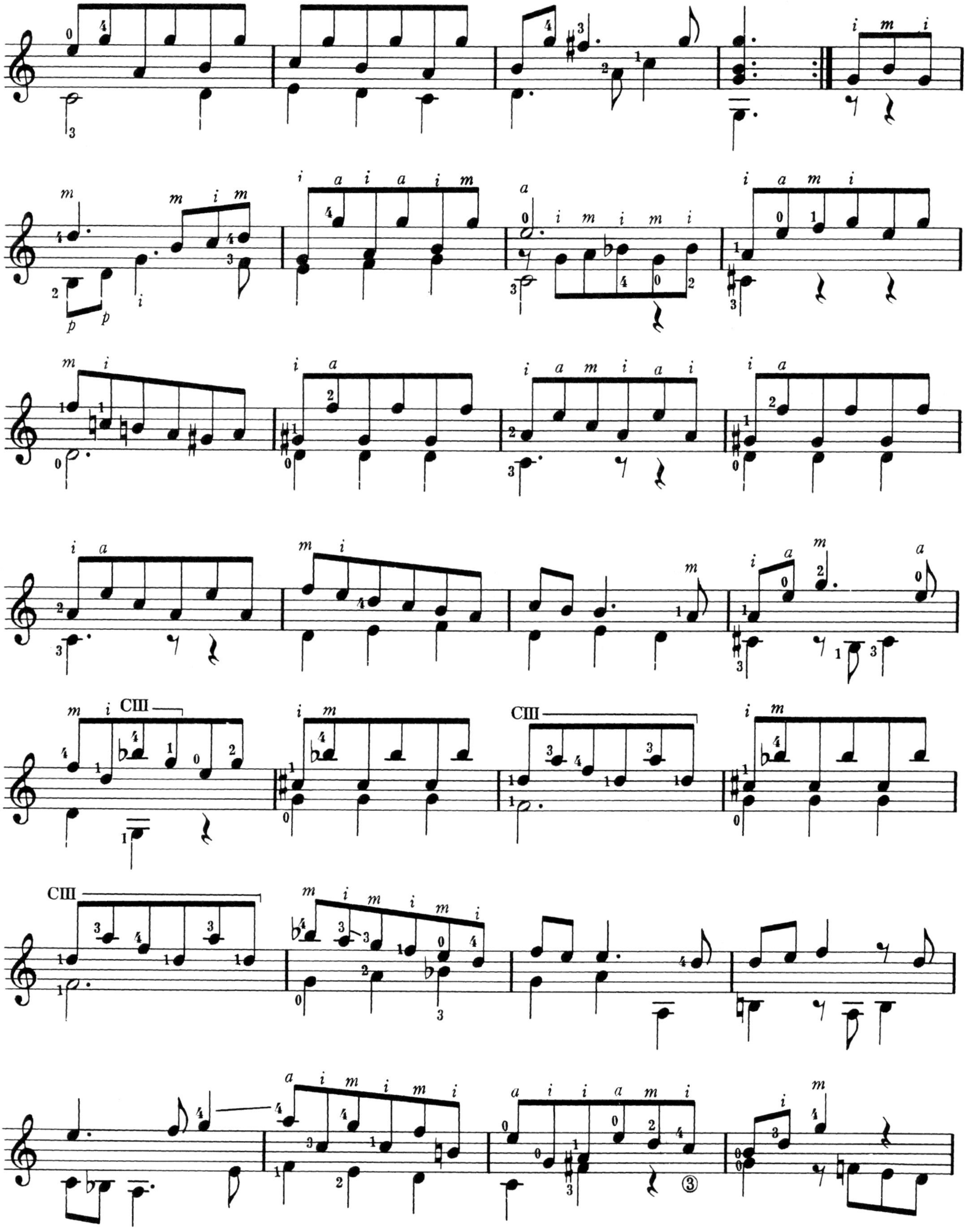
CIII
CIII
CIII

SLEEPER'S AWAKE

This well-known and excellent chorale closes Cantata Number 140, "Wachet auf, ruft uns die Stimme." The translation would read: "Awake! the voice is calling to us." This composition is often played on the organ, the chorale theme appearing within an inner part. Continuous embellishment is provided in the upper part, played by the right hand.

The tempo should be a comfortable Andante. Be sure to play all grace notes on the beat, that is, at the same time as the bass note.

Andante commodo

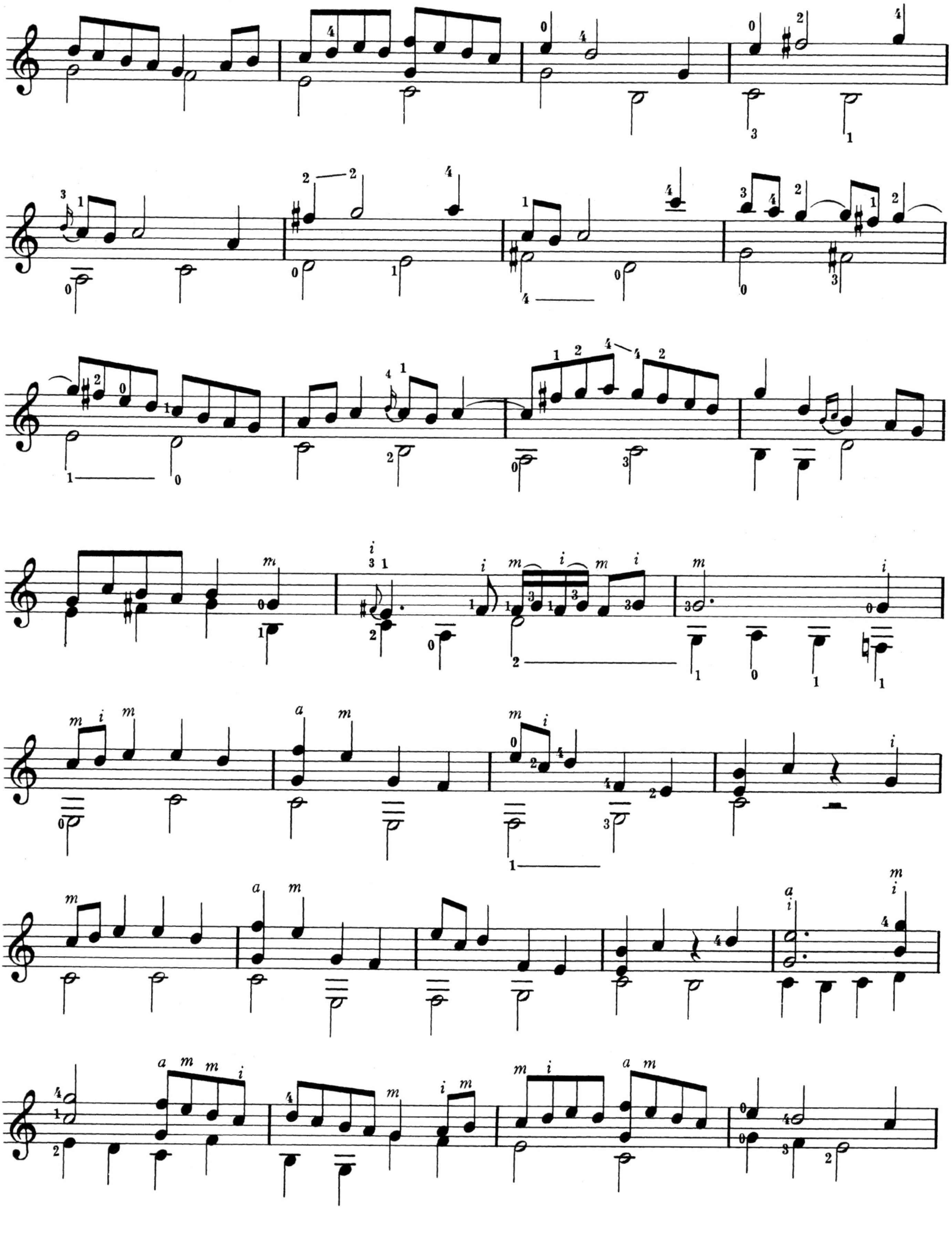

AIR FOR THE G STRING

This piece has a double identity. The first is simply "Air" and as such constitutes one of the slow movements of Bach's "Suite #3 in D Major" for small orchestra. The second identity, "Air For The G String" is the more familiar and came about as a result of August Wilhelmj's arrangement of it for violin and piano. Wilhelmj, who lived from 1845 to 1908, was a famous concert violinist. His arrangement is in C Major and that key has been retained for this transcription. It might be well to remember that the moving bass part is played pizzicato on string basses in the orchestral version. The grace notes that appear are to be played on the beat.

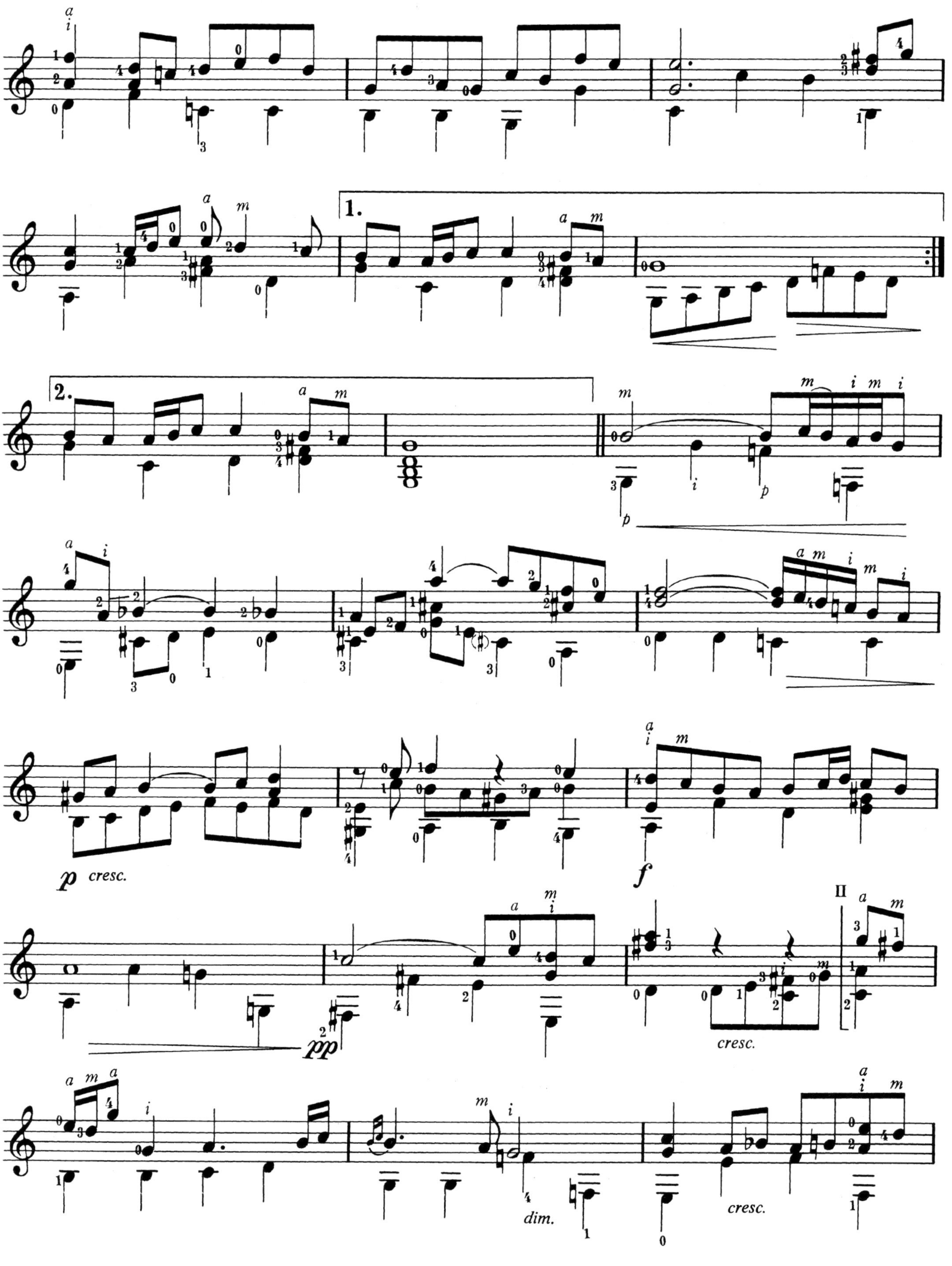
1.
2.
p cresc.
f
pp
cresc.
II
dim.
cresc.

GAVOTTE
from 6th Sonata for Solo Violin

The record of the Bach family of musicians in the history of music is unparalleled. The Bachs, without intermission, were making music in Germany from the age of Luther (1483-1546) to the time of Bismark (1815-1898). In a letter to a friend dated 1730, Bach says: "All my children are born musicians. I can already form a concert, vocal and instrumental in my own family." Besides the musical parents, there were twenty children.

A Gavotte is a French dance. A characteristic of gavottes is that they start on the up beat of the opening measure. The tempo is moderately fast. The grace notes are played on the beat.

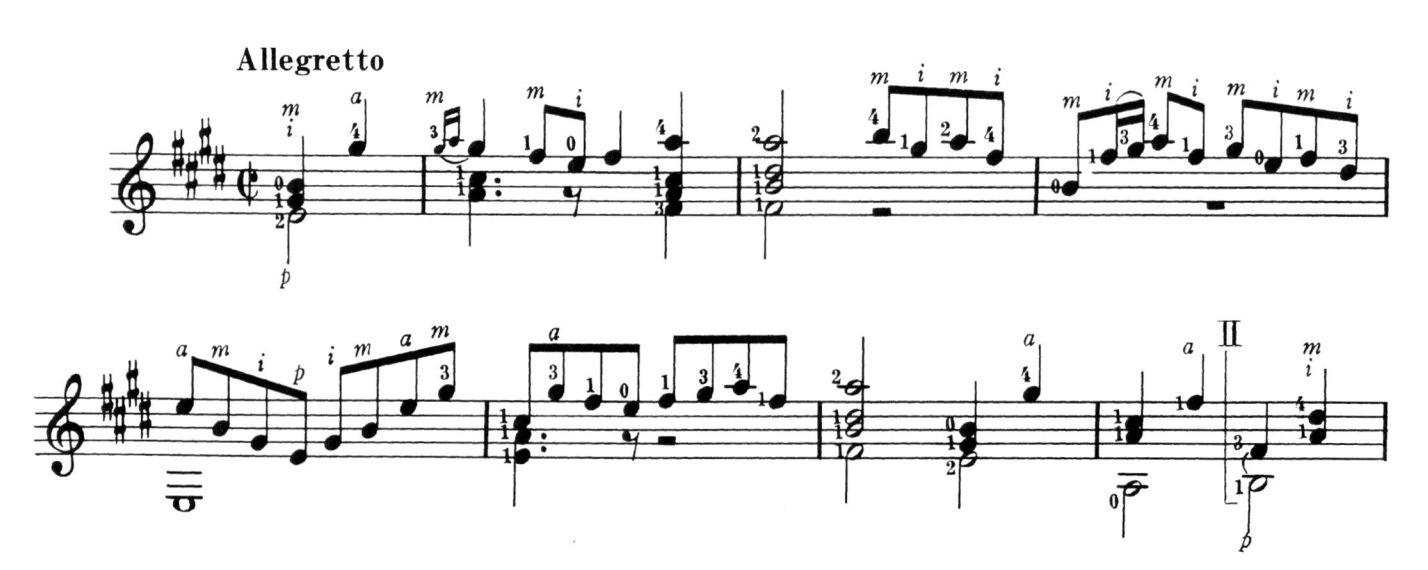

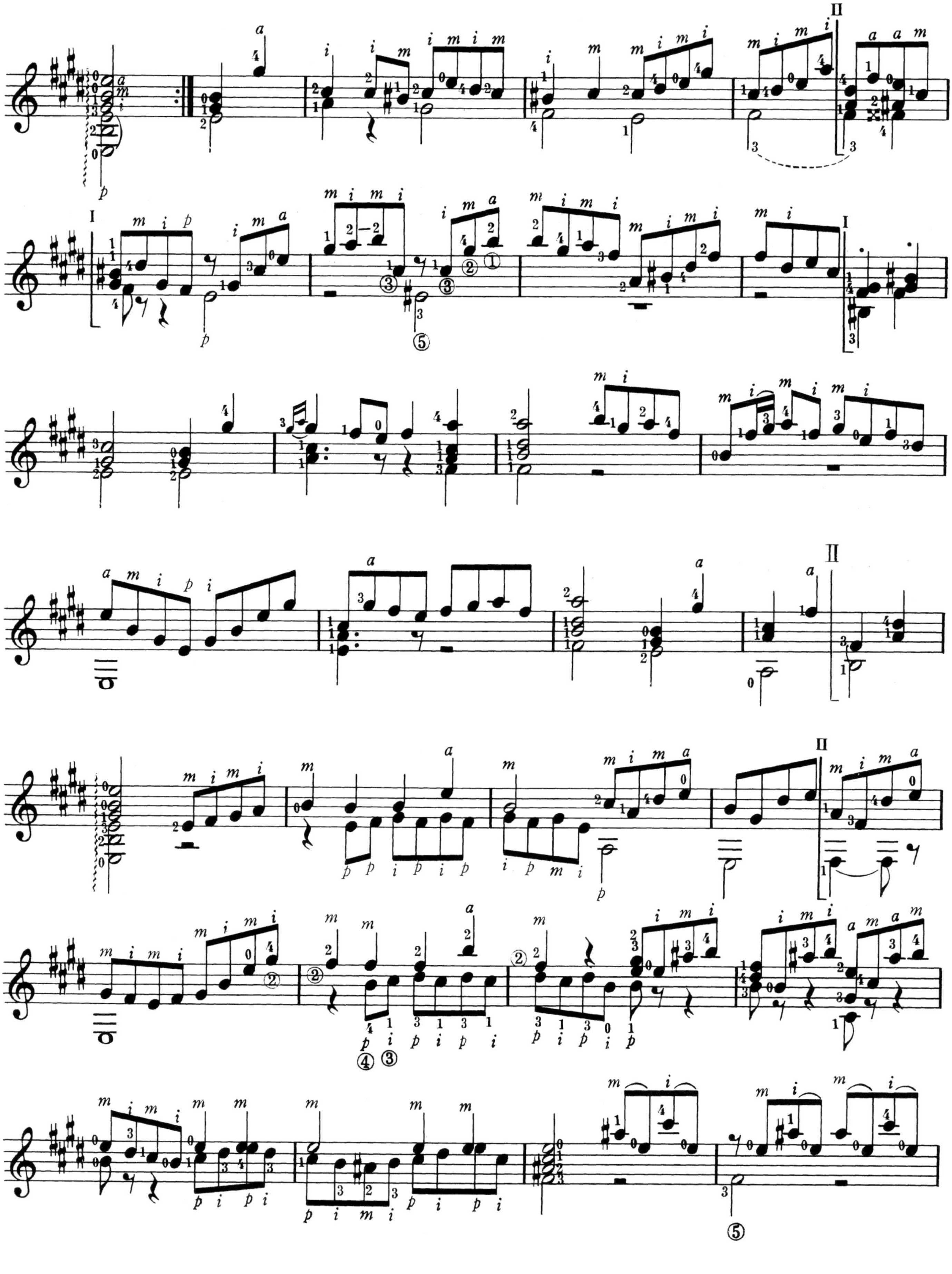

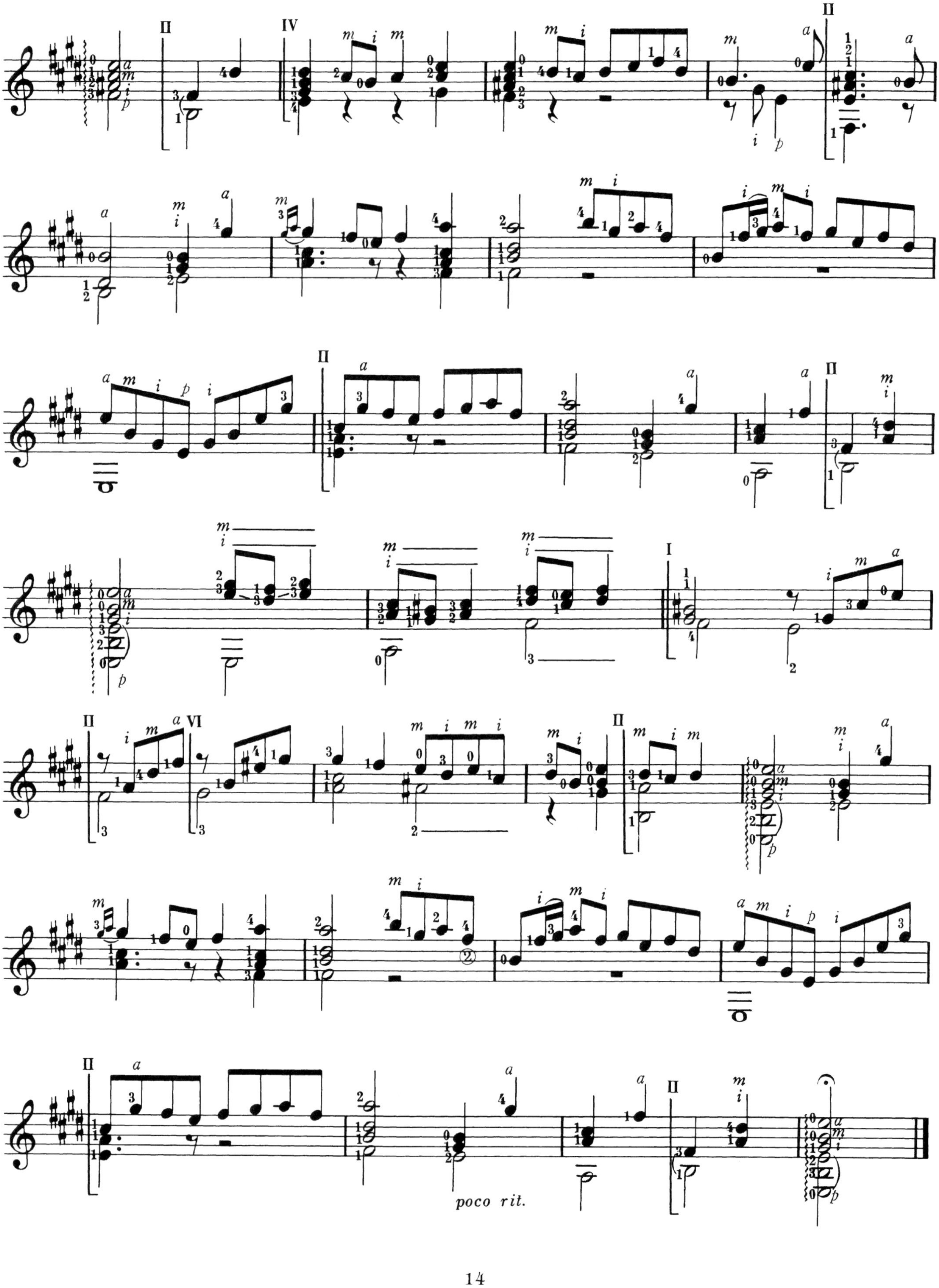
poco rit.

COURANTE
from Suite No. 3 for Cello

Johann Sebastian Bach
(1685–1750)

Allegro moderato

16

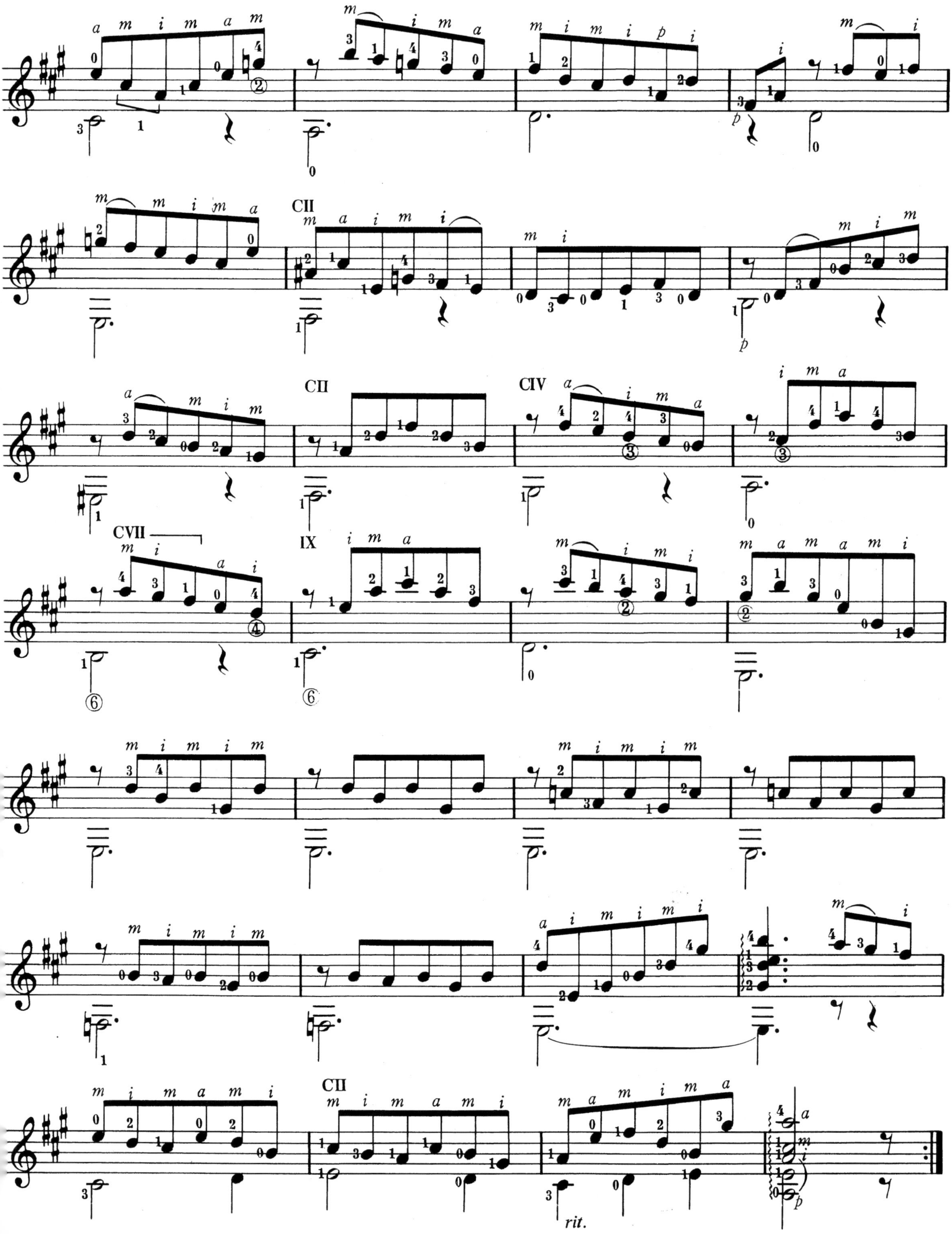
CII
CII
CIV
CVII
IX
CII
rit.